# Jin Can Fly



by Tim Little
Illustrated by Bill Ledger

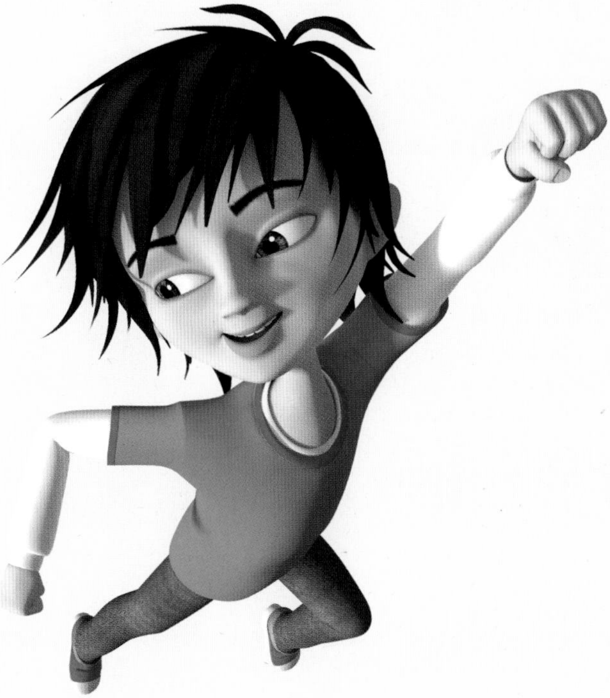

OXFORD
UNIVERSITY PRESS

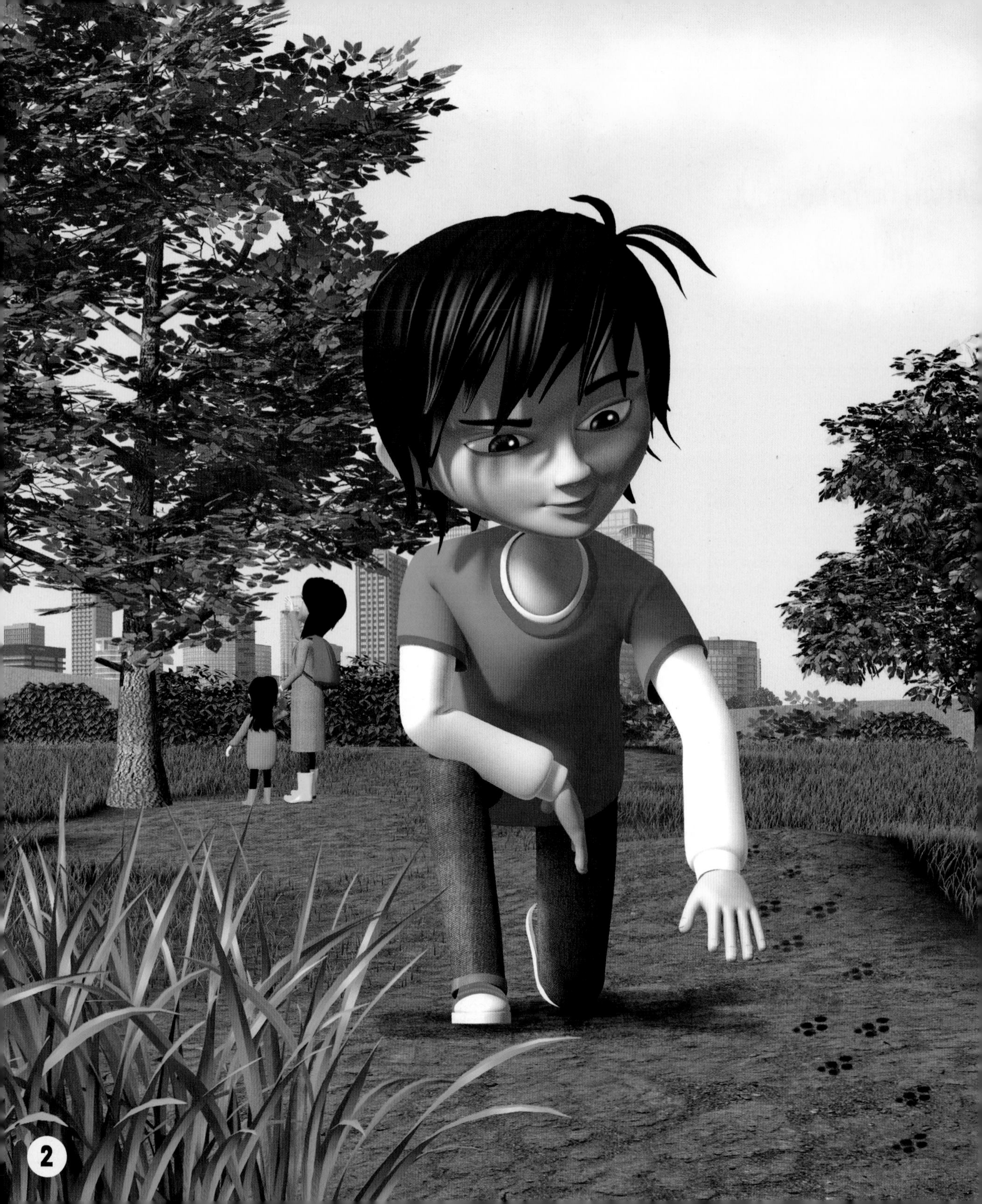

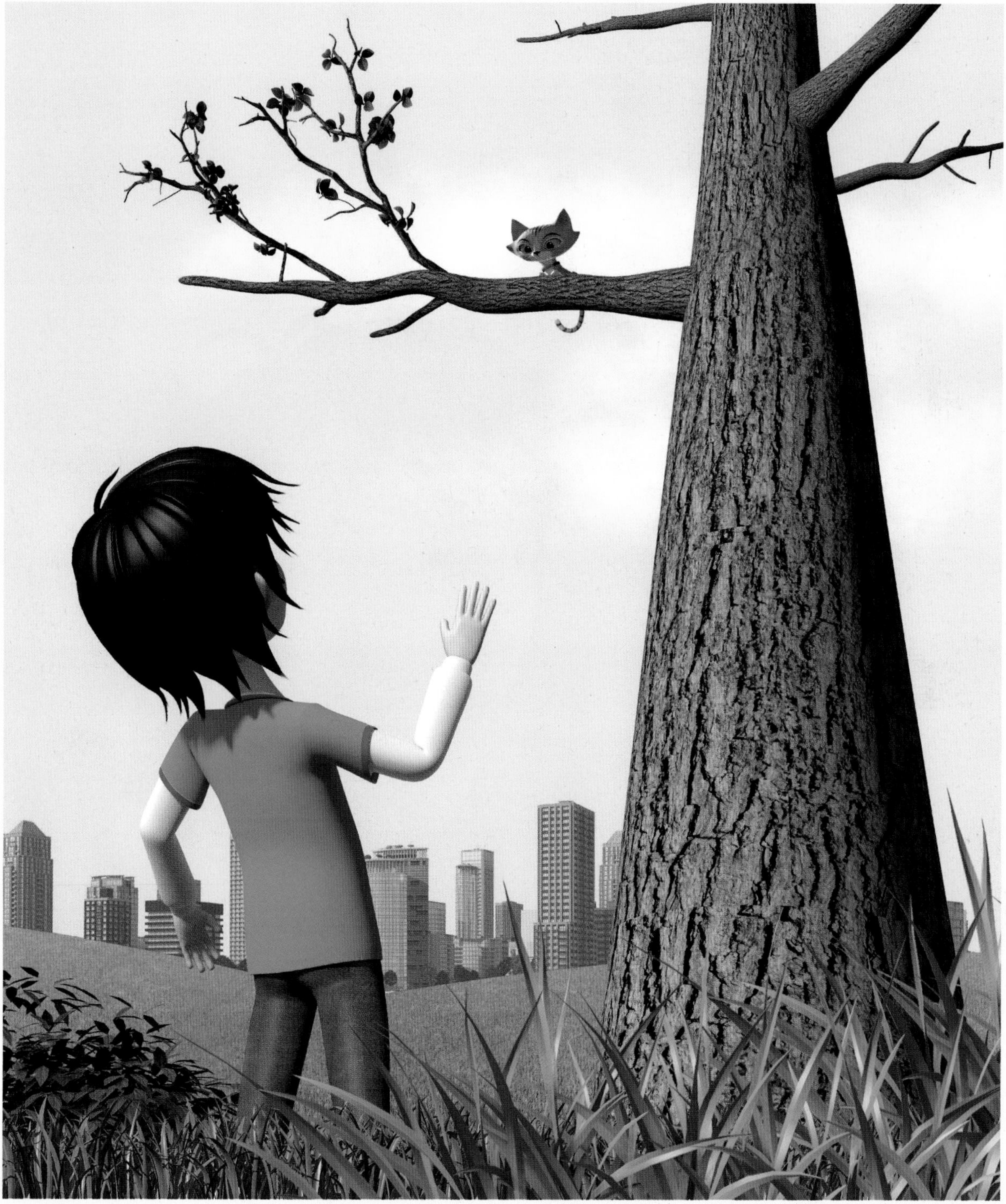

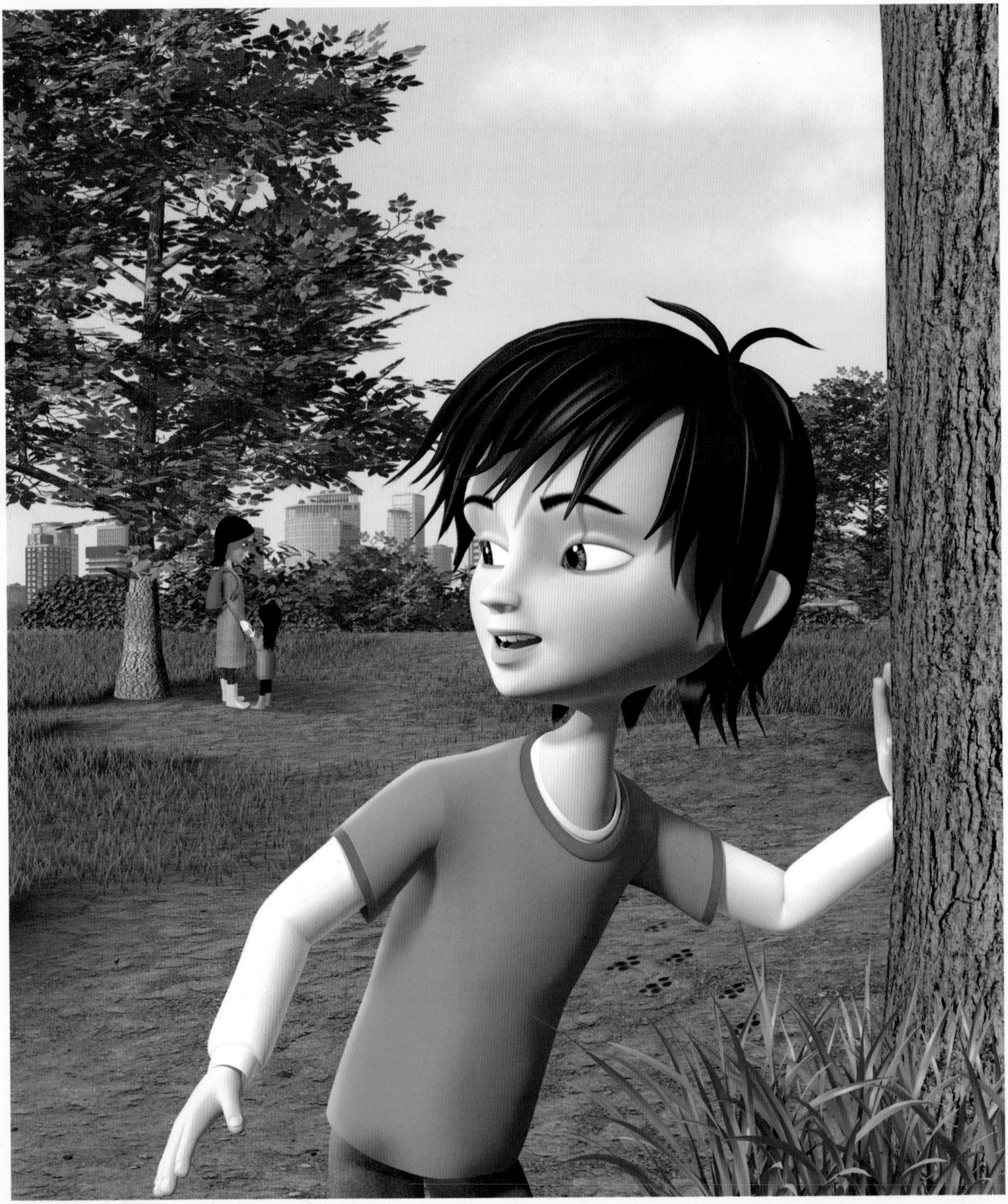

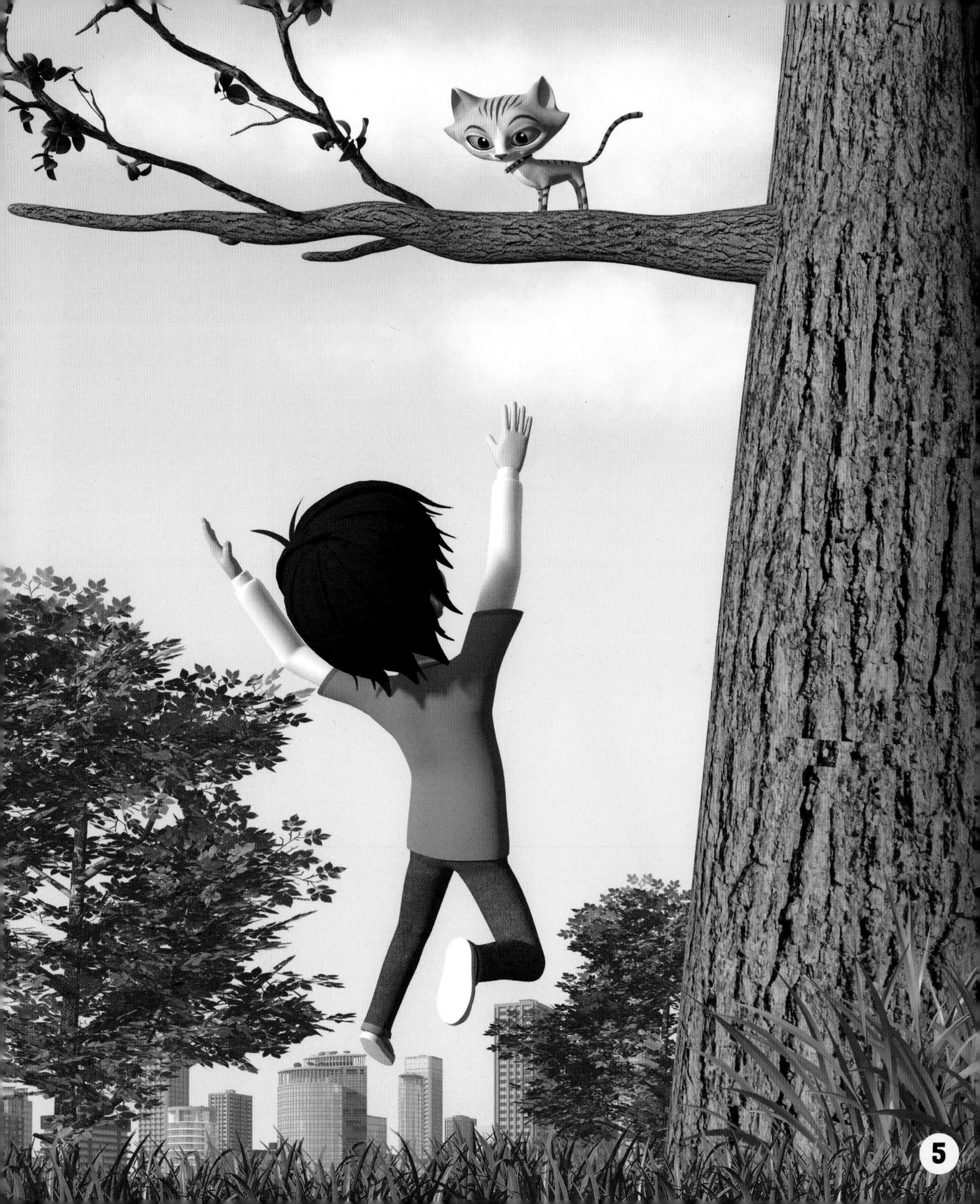

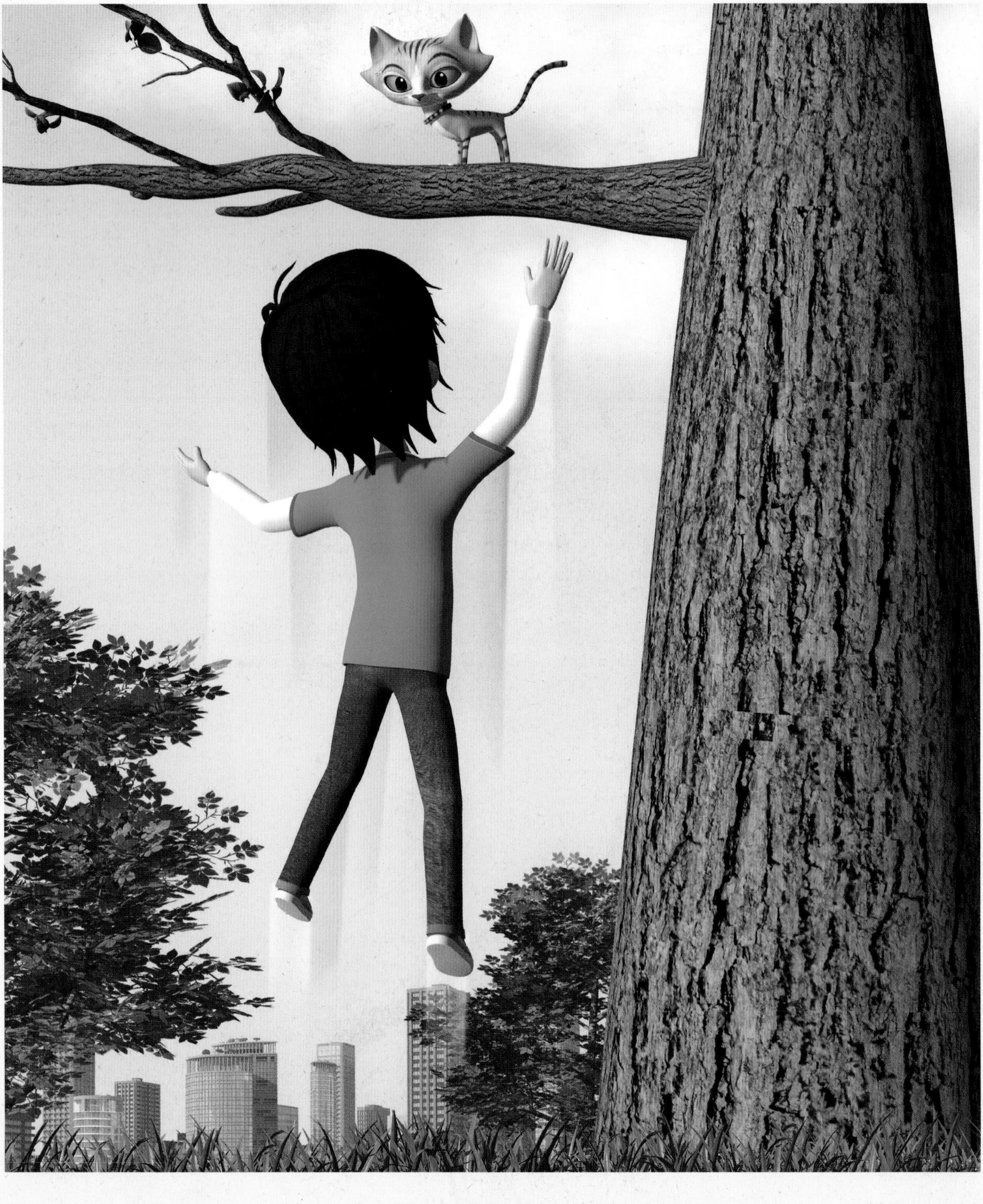

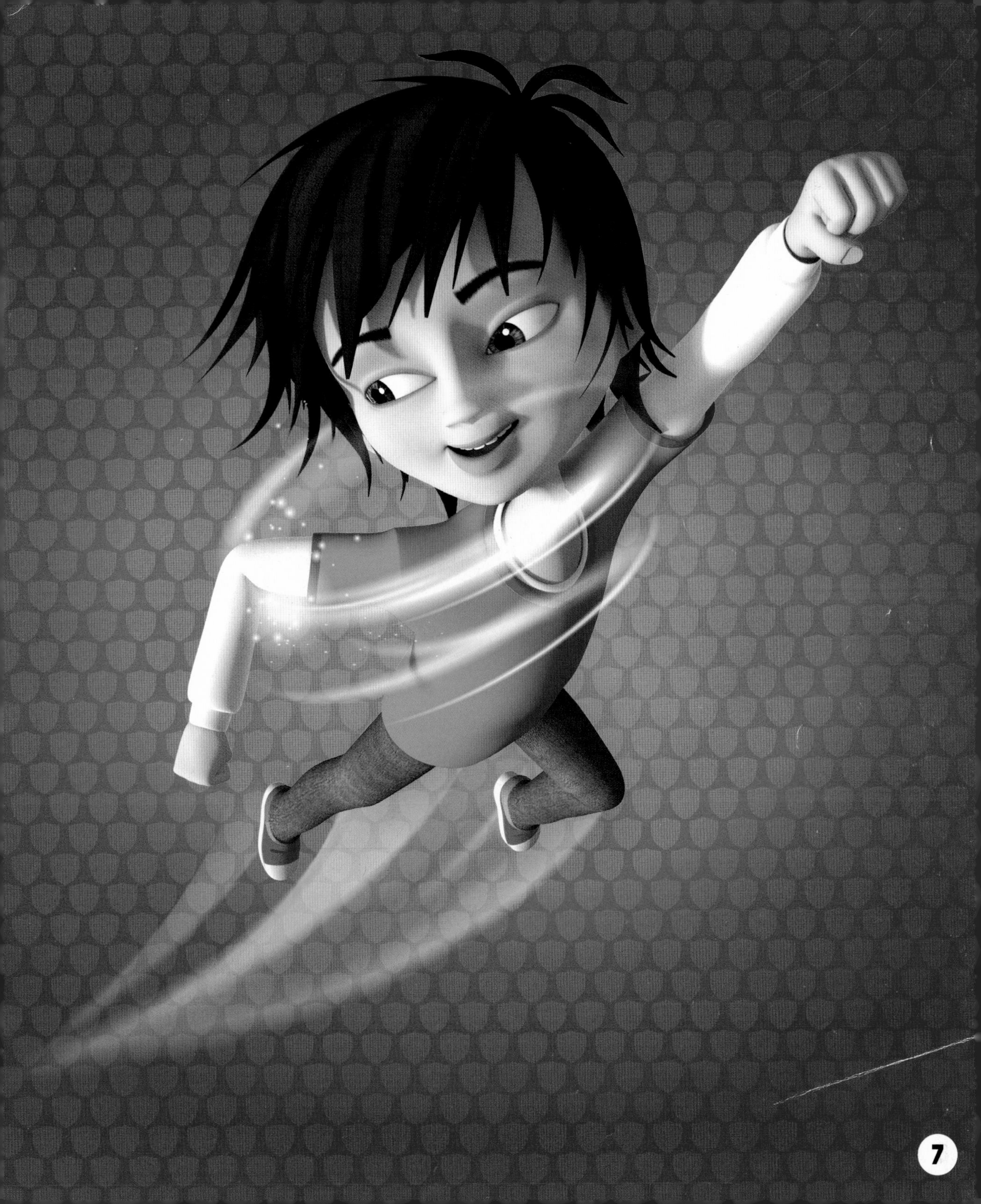

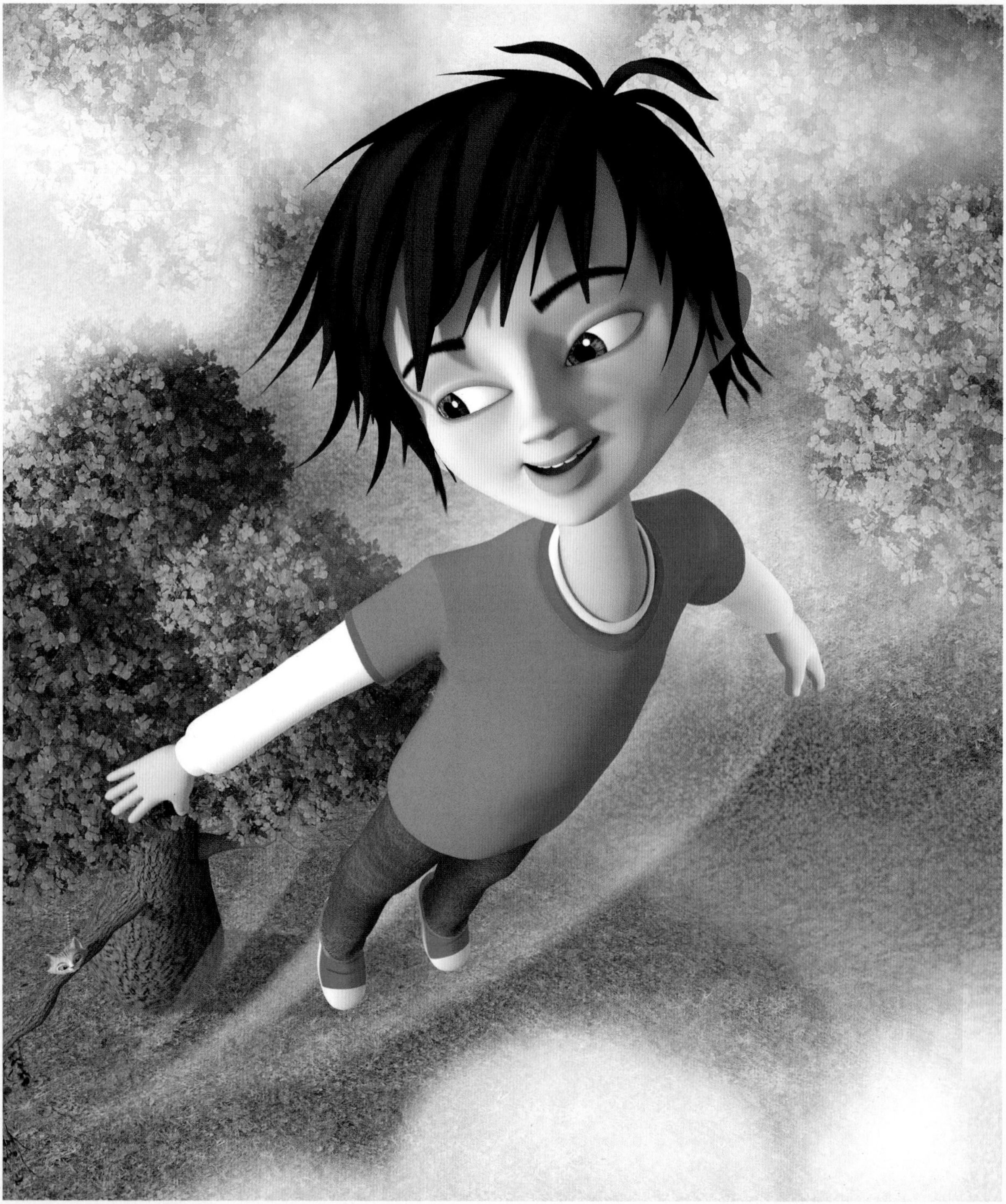

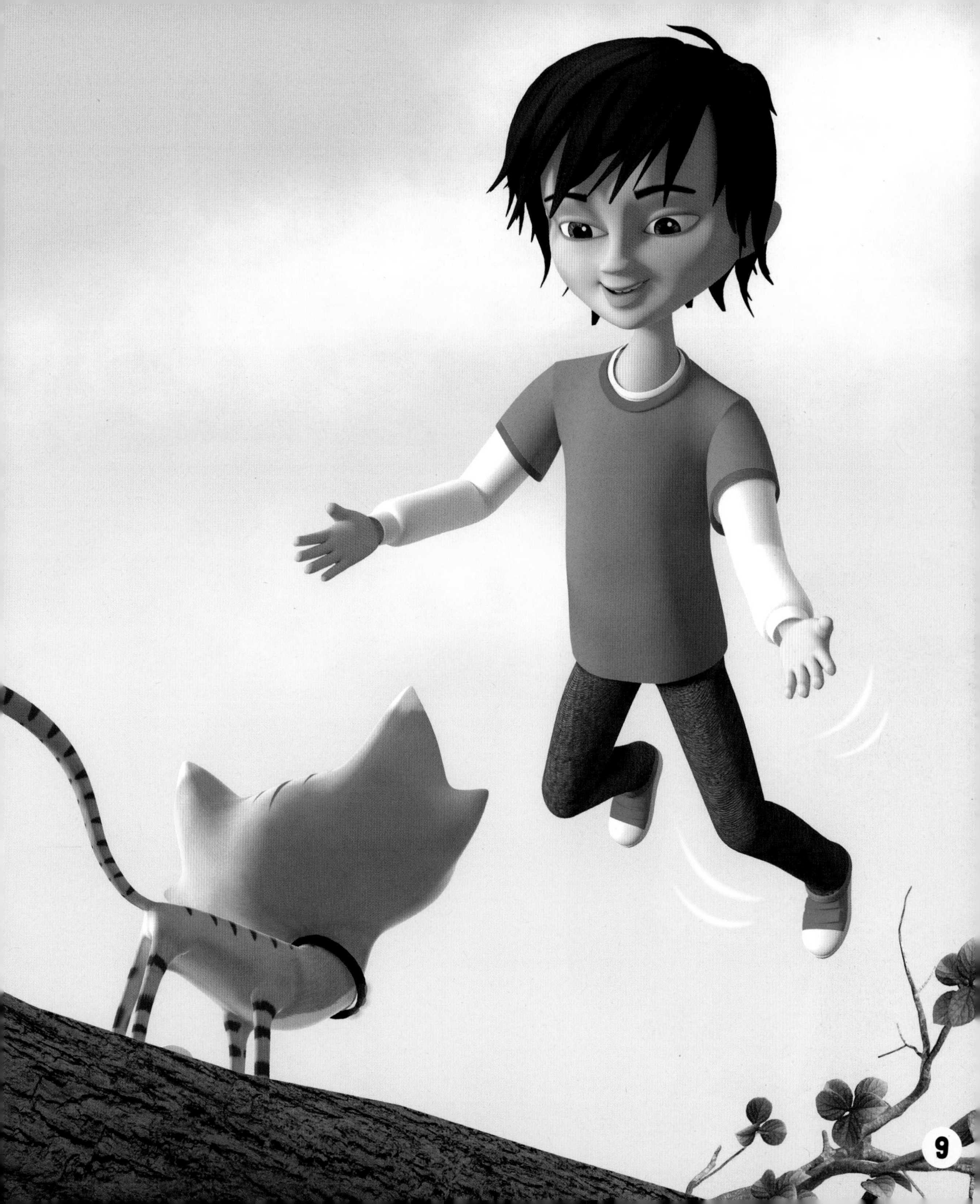

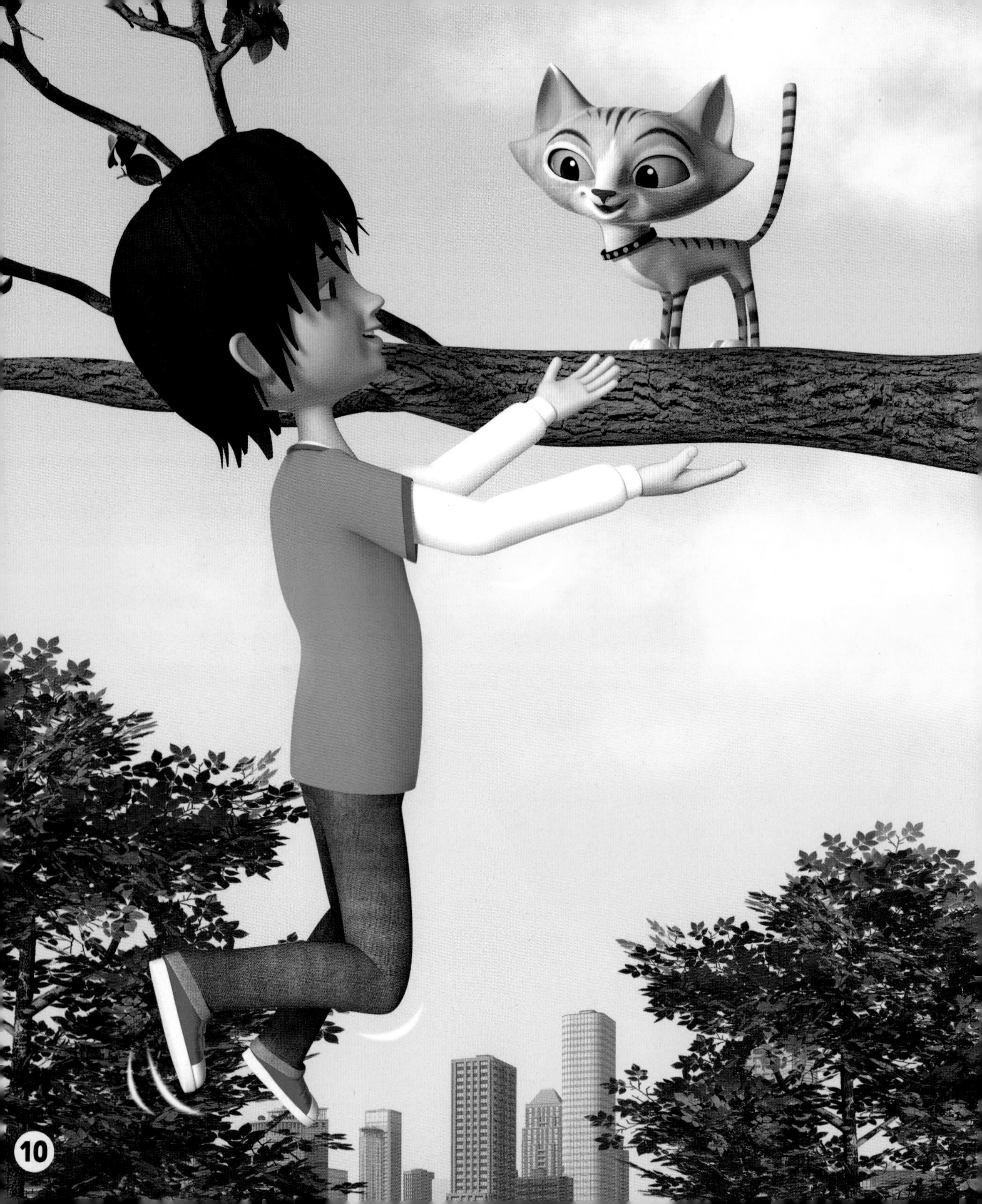

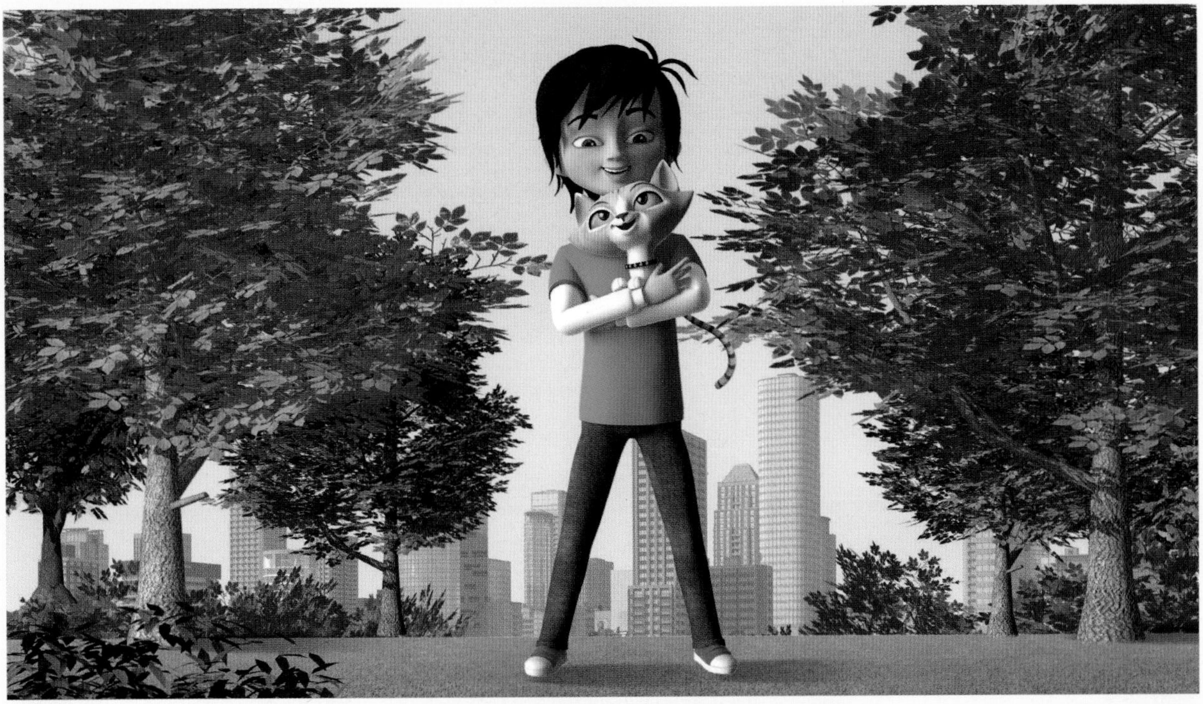

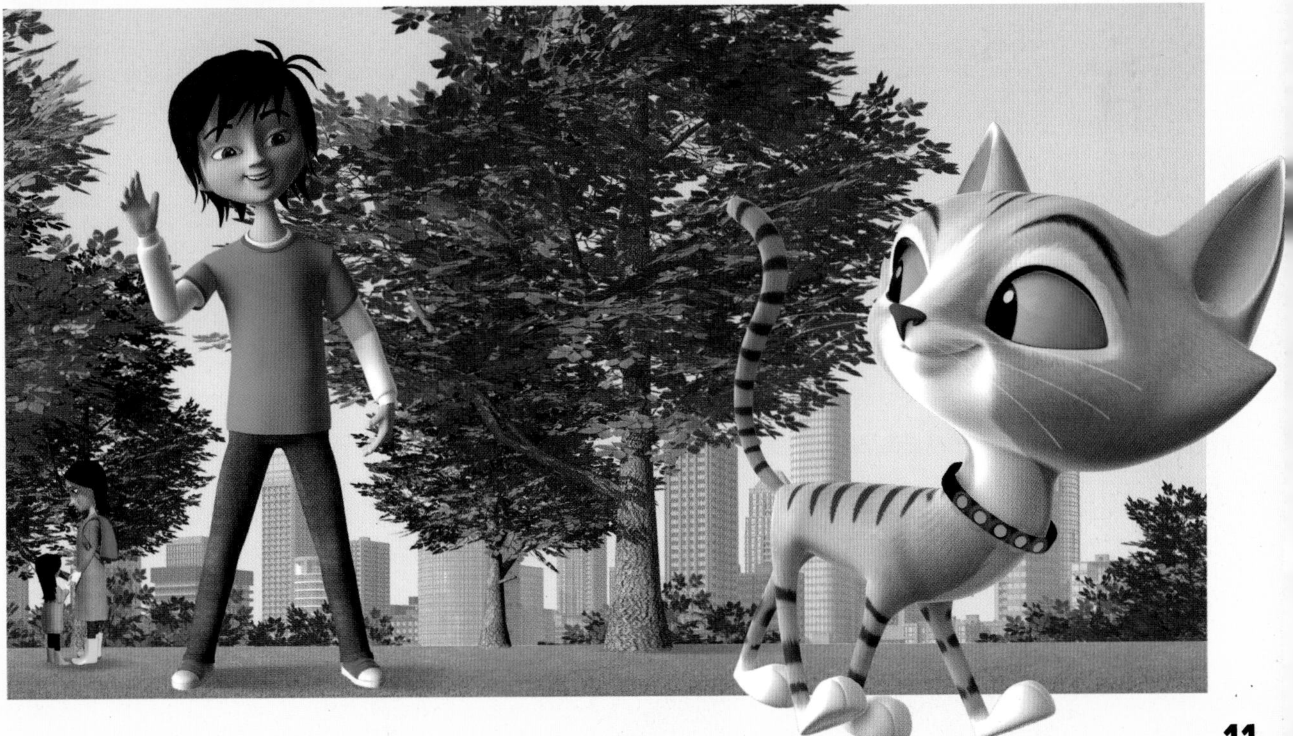

# Retell the story ...

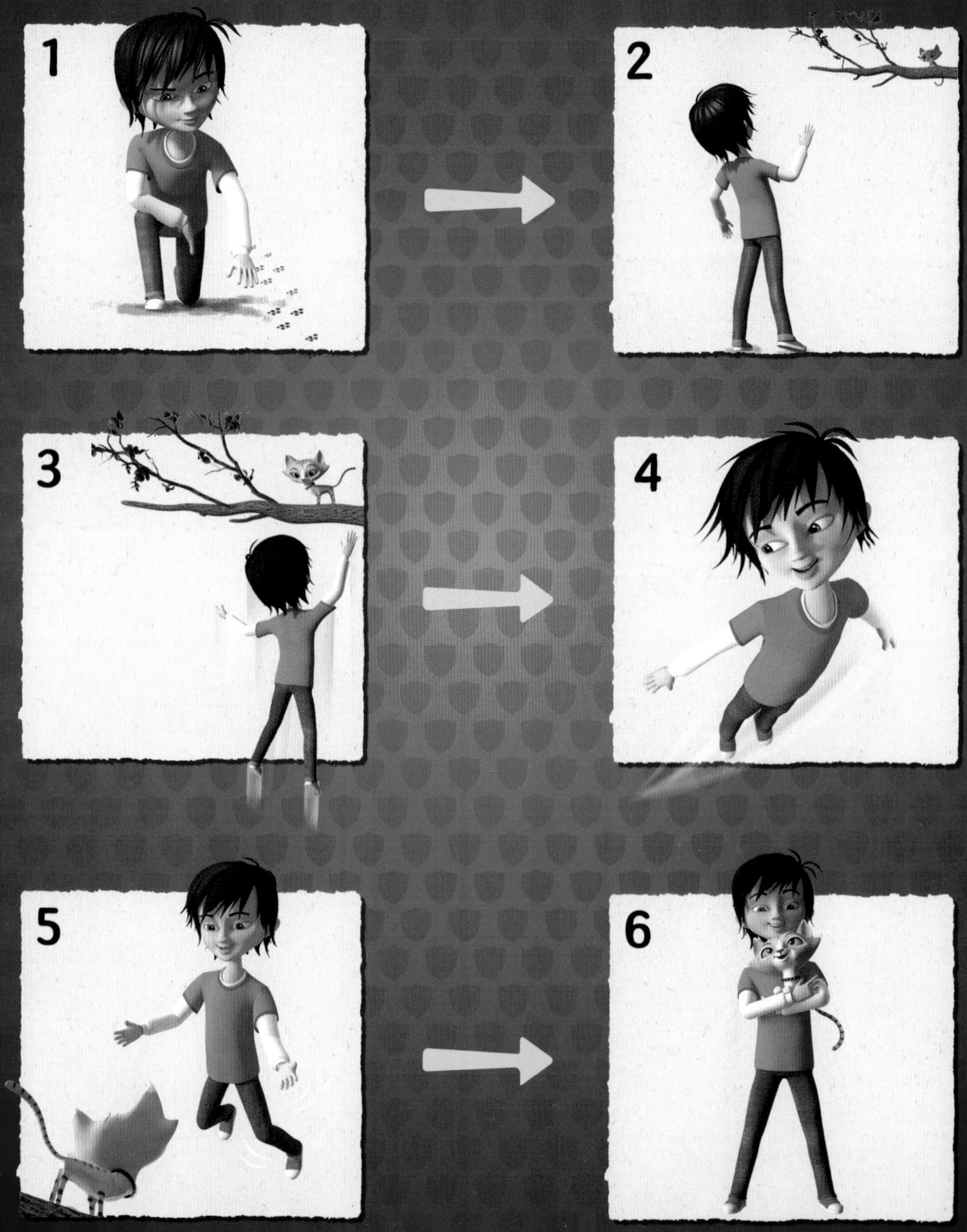